The Glorious Church The Bride

Robert F Paden and The Plowman

Published by The Plowman, 2022.

While every precaution has been taken in the preparation of this book, the publisher assumes no responsibility for errors or omissions, or for damages resulting from the use of the information contained herein.

THE GLORIOUS CHURCH THE BRIDE

First edition. September 21, 2022.

Copyright © 2022 Robert F Paden and The Plowman.

ISBN: 979-8215516508

Written by Robert F Paden and The Plowman.

Table of Contents

From each one of my teachers, I have learned something; form
my students as well. The Bible puts everything into perspective.
But most of all, I dedicate this book to the Lord Jesus Christ
who makes all things work together for good.

CHAPTER ONE
The Battle for the Kingdom

God is not limited to time or space as we are nor is He just like us "but a lot bigger". Nor is God <u>like</u> all the power of the universe, He <u>created</u> all the power of the universe. I like the song that Andy Griffin sings, "Somebody bigger than you and I" And <u>yet,</u> in his love He did make us a little bit like himself! And not only that, God's main purpose and design all through the Bible is to form a people! A people of sons and daughters like his son Jesus! And He dearly wants each of us to be a part of that people, a "people called out (from the world) after his own name". And He will dwell right in our midst! Not only in our midst but also to share our life with each one of us! What great lengths God went to form a people of children like Jesus! He sent his Son Jesus (his only begotten and dearly beloved son) to live with us. Jesus left heaven, put off his power and might, put off his majesty, and came to live among us! He walked with us and lived with us. He struggled with us and for us, but he overcame, So that "in his name" and by the power of his Spirit in us, we might be like him and also overcome!

Just imagine, He who <u>made the universe</u> *walked in sandals*! He got his feet dirty and got tired, just like us! He was tempted, just like us, but without sin! He was the perfect example of a man. He fulfilled all righteousness and overcame every evil. Satan tried to sidetrack him or trick him or pressure him into avoiding the cross. But Jesus answered the lies and half lies of Satan with the truth of the Scriptures. The master of lies showed Jesus all the kingdoms of this world and offered him the power over them. He said "For they have been *delivered* unto me". Jesus did not dispute his claim, but He said, "**It is written**, you shall worship the Lord your God, and Him only shall you serve."

Who had delivered all the kingdoms of this world to Satan? It was Adam! God had given Adam <u>dominion</u> over all the earth and every living thing upon the earth. So, when Adam gave in to the temptations of Satan, in effect he bowed down before him and delivered that dominion to Satan. The apostle Paul calls Satan the prince of the power of the air. He got that power by deceiving Adam to hand it over to him! But Jesus did not give in to Satan nor think for one moment on taking a short cut to setting up a new kingdom, but commanded Satan to get behind him! *God does not change his mind just to make things easier.* He had given this authority to man and man had delivered it unto Satan's hand, so it was necessary that a <u>man</u> take it back. But since ordinary man was now Satan's slave, and a slave has no power over his master, it was now necessary that a man, a **perfect man** take back from Satan that authority. Later we see that Jesus "<u>bound the strong man and spoiled his house</u>!"

As Jesus began to minister and his popularity grew, this world system (Satan's kingdom) rose up against him in the form of the Pharisees and Sadducees and even his own brothers doubted him at first. Our Lord, who opened the way for us, <u>the way that we should go</u>, overcame this world system. He fulfilled <u>all the will of God for man</u> and recovered what man had lost. God had in the beginning, given authority over his creation to man, but all Adam's unborn children *died spiritually* as he bowed down to Satan's hand! The loss was incalculable!

Then God's creatures cried out for help, but there was no permanent help given them until Jesus came! The great man Job prophetically cried out, "For He (God) is not a man as I am that I should answer him, and we should come together in judgment. *Oh that there was an arbiter between us,* to put his hand both of us!" The Almighty and holy God was unreachable by man, now estranged from God and under Satan's deceitful power. So how profound a statement it is that Jesus "<u>bound the strong man and spoiled his house</u>!" He is that <u>arbiter</u> that put his hand on both of us! He bridged that tremendous gap between God and man made by sin. And how tremendous it is that he (Jesus) has given us (the church) power over all the power of the enemy (Satan and his minions)!

But the church has no spiritual power of its own; it only has the power of Jesus, though it can have <u>all</u> the power of Jesus! We can't say that it <u>does</u> have all the power of Jesus but that it <u>can</u> have all that power. Jesus said, "Where (even) two or three are gathered together <u>in my name</u>, there am I in the midst of them!" We must examine the meaning of this statement carefully, because where Jesus is, there is his power, and he has been given **all authority in heaven and earth**. <u>There is no power greater than his</u>. There is no enemy that can even confront him. All the demons cower and run at the mention of his name! But then in reality, why doesn't the church always have this power? It even seems that some churches never have this power! He said, when they are <u>gathered in my name</u>! Could it be that sometimes though we tag on to our prayers, "in the name of Jesus, amen", that we are not really gathered in his name?

Let's say that an important business man wants to start a new enterprise far from his home base. He picks a man in whom he puts his trust to do all of his will in this new area with his new enterprise. The man has authority to hire or fire people, to pay their wages, to buy materials, to write checks, to buy land, all <u>in the name</u> of his employer. But if this administrator decides to do his own enterprise with his employer's money, his boss will soon find out and take away his authority because not to do the perfect will of his employer was not to do it <u>in his name</u>!

CHRISTIANS GATHER together to have a good time. That's not bad, but often they are not really interested in doing the will of their Lord at that moment. The green jokes start to flow, the good beer keeps being served up. The barbecue was great and the "fellowship" even greater during the evening as time slipped away. They got home pretty late and next morning, Sunday they didn't get up in time to make it to church. "But we can worship God at home can't we?" They said. "The preacher won't mind. He knows its summer and many of the folks are having vacations and other activities. Besides, didn't we have fellowship with brethren last night. That's what it's all about isn't it?"

Ok, let's you and I be honest about it. Were they really gathered in the Lord's name? Were they really doing the will of our Holy Father? Why is there no power? Many are saying Lord, Lord with their mouths but their heart is far from him. They are not always gathering together in the Lord's name, even when they come to the Sunday meeting. They may have the best music group in town, the finest sound system, the most eloquent preacher and still not have a clue what God wants to do in their lives. They have what you might call a comfortable religion. Everything is in order according to the order of service and they <u>know they will get out on time</u>.

JESUS SAID, "You have given me a body! *I come to do your will, oh God*!" and the apostle Paul exhorted us to "present our bodies a <u>living sacrifice</u>, holy, acceptable unto our God, which is your <u>reasonable</u> service." And then prophesied that "there will come a time when they will not endure sound doctrine; but after their own lusts shall they heap to themselves teachers, having itching ears. And they shall turn away their ears from the truth, and shall be turned unto fables." And "in the last days perilous times shall come" but "all that will live godly in Christ Jesus shall suffer persecution".

IN PERSPECTIVE we see the glorious church! The apostle Peter said, "of which salvation, (that Jesus purchased for us) the prophets have enquired and searched diligently, who prophesied of the grace that should come unto you, searching what, or what manner of time the Spirit of Christ which was in them did signify when it testified beforehand the sufferings of Christ, and the **glory** that should follow!" He was talking about us, about our time, about the church of today! And the apostle Paul prayed "That the God of our Lord Jesus Christ, the Father of glory, may give unto you the spirit of wisdom and revelation in the *knowledge of him* (and that) the eyes of your understanding be enlightened that you may know what is the *hope of his calling*, and what the *riches of the glory of his inheritance in the saints*. And what is the *exceeding greatness of his power* to us ward who believe according to the working of his mighty power, which He wrought in **Christ, when he raised him from the dead,** and set him at his own right hand in the heavenly places <u>far above all principality and power and might, and dominion and every name that is named not only in this world, but also in that which is to come,</u> and has put *all* things under his feet, and gave him to be the head over all things <u>to the *church,*</u> which is his body, *the fullness* of him that fills all in all!" (Eph 1: 17-23)

Can we understand all that? God has given to the church the same power that raised Christ Jesus from the dead! And He has put all things under the feet of Jesus and the church is the body of Jesus so all things are under the feet of the church. How glorious is that?

The primitive church, submersed in the love of God, incentivized by the vision Jesus had given them and by the knowledge of his resurrection, and empowered by his Holy Spirit, preached the gospel to much of the civilized world in just one generation. Phrases like; "Those that have turned the world upside down have come hither also!" and "all those that dwelt in Asia heard the word of the Lord Jesus, both Jews and Greeks" and "Therefore they that were scattered abroad (by the persecution) went everywhere preaching the word." All of which give us a clue of the excitement and courage and power that the early church had! (Acts 17:6, 19:10, - 8:4-5)

Paul exhorted his disciples in Philippi to be "nothing terrified by your adversaries: which is to them an evident token of perdition, but to you of salvation, and that of God." A good part of the glory of the early church was the courage and selflessness of the disciples to literally give their lives to bring salvation to those that hadn't heard.

The Church has manifested its glory many times down through the ages, especially during times of severe persecution. When persecution came from the Roman Empire, on their first reaction, Christians many times failed but as the persecution grew more severe, so the glory of the church began to manifest itself as fearless martyrs laid down their lives rather than give away their faith. In Revelation 12 it tells the story of many brave Christians from all the ages who overcame the devil "by the blood of the Lamb and by the word of their testimony and that they *loved not their lives unto the death.*" It is said that the secretary of Nero, the demented emperor who attempted to exterminate Christians, said to him, "Your Excellency, the more Christians we kill, the more that appear! It seems that in order to rid ourselves of the Christians, we shall have to kill all of Rome!"

But when the emperor Constantine converted to Christianity and declared the whole Roman Empire Christian, the power of politics and money subverted the church and over time almost the entire church lost its power. What Satan could not accomplish from outside the church, he did very nicely once he got inside! For a thousand years human progress was almost halted and the entire world was plunged into darkness because the light of the world (the church) was darkened. Even secular history books speak of the "dark ages".

But there were those in every age that carried the torch (of whom the world was not worthy). The world does not know many of their names but God does! John Huss from Bohemia and John Wycliffe from England both taught the Word of God from the Bible. John Huss was burned at the stake. Many who stood by their faith paid a very high price. Martin Luther, many who followed in his footsteps and those who tried to make the Bible available to the common man risked their very lives. Many became martyrs.

THE CHURCH DIDN'T DIE and the Word of God didn't die. We come to more recent history. Carl Marx, the son of a Jewish Christian family. He was sent away to study and at first, he wrote Christian prose, but at a turning point in his life, he wrote, "See this sword? I purchased it from the Prince of Darkness!" From that point on he began to write for Satan himself. In his writings the struggle of the working people evolved into "The Communist Manifesto". This was an *imitation* of the social good will in the Church in Jerusalem ordered by the Lord to provide for all the people who were visiting Jerusalem during the feast of Pentecost and stayed to learn the new walk in the Kingdom of Christ after the infilling of the Holy Spirit.

Not only was Communism an imitation of Christians, Carl Marx denied the Lord and as he was now serving Satan, he and his followers taught that God didn't exist. Communism spread all over Eastern Europe (and from there to China). They taught that the end justifies the means and with that doctrine killed and tortured any who would dare to get in their way or who belonged to a class of people who might get in their way. It is estimated that the Bolshevik revolution and the later Communist regime killed over <u>100 million people</u>. Some have even put that figure at 175 million. Their goal was to dominate the world. It seemed that nothing would stop them!

But there was a little power inside the Soviet Union, a little light. They tried to put it out! They tortured and killed and put in prison all pastors and Christian workers who would not bow to their regime. They taught in the schools daily that there is no God! They paid spies in every neighborhood to report any Christian activity. God was dead; they said they had killed him! They had killed the church——-they thought!

But slowly, very slowly as the decadent church died the *glorious church* began to appear. Small witnesses, here and there, very scattered. One prisoner speaking a word to another, "Jesus is the answer!" Persecutors were sent to destroy any Christian meeting that they could find, but the persecuted bore witness to the persecutors! Some were converted! In Poland the people raise up a cross and the government tears it down, again and again until the government gives up and lets them have their cross! In Russia a catholic priest continually encouraged his people to trust in Christ. They tortured and killed him, but could not kill the faith that he inspired. Though it wasn't manifest to the outside world, God was answering the prayers of his saints both inside and outside the Communist Regime. In Romania, a young man began to preach fiery sermons and inspire the people. Many people began to come to his meetings from all walks of life and spiritual backgrounds.

The regime oppose that church and try to stop their meetings. They resist and resist the regime, and one night in the city square of Timisoara, Romania, the <u>people resist the army</u>. Many die, but they keep singing the gospel and freedom and marching forward till the army stops shooting. The Communist dictator flees in a helicopter. Not only the government, but the very history of Romania is changed overnight!

These things happen all over the great Soviet Union. And then one day, the entire evil empire <u>collapses.</u> The tearing down of the Berlin wall was just a physical symbol of what had happened all through that evil empire., There were certainly other factors, such as President Ronald Reagan's resolute resistance which our sovereign God ordained to hold the USSR in check, but what destroyed the Soviet Union from inside was the *glorious church*. The world didn't know nor will ever admit that the glorious church destroyed that evil empire without firing a shot!

MAO TSE TUNG helped form the Communist party in China and led the revolution that took over China in 1948-49. They tried in every way to stamp out Christianity imprisoning, torturing killing and outlawing Christianity and Christians. The "bamboo curtain" closed so tightly that from outside, we thought perhaps Christianity was dead in China. The missionaries were expelled. The pastors and all Christian leaders were tortured and imprisoned or killed. Churches were outlawed. <u>For thirty-five years</u> the outside world had no knowledge of what was happening inside.

When the "bamboo curtain" closed there were an estimated 750,000 Christians in China, a very tiny minority in a country of nearly a billion people. In 1983, thirty-five years later, Mao was dead and the curtain began to open. Would there be any Christians left? The Christians of the world were on tip toe, waiting to see if any Christians survived. Many even thought that perhaps the missionaries had preached a "dead" gospel, one that had no power. Perhaps there would be no witness left proclaiming the gospel. To our great surprise and delight, the brothers and sister who were carrying Bibles into that tortured land found that the Christian church had multiplied! Had it ever multiplied! Christians were everywhere, in every walk of life. Business men, peasants, coulees and school teachers. Yes, they had multiplied. It was then estimated that there were over 7 million Christians and still growing! The hunger for Bibles was insatiable. The government still outlawed Christianity, but could not contain it!

But this was all bought at a terrible price. The church of China made a video of their history. Many told of suffering and death at the hands of the communists. We don't know how many died. Many leaders that survived had spent 20 years in prison and suffering. Some had been imprisoned several times. One old man who had spent many years in and out of prison, decided to build his house near the prison door and there proclaim Christ as Savior! They couldn't silence him, having imprisoned him many times. They finally began telling everyone that he was crazy but the common people held him in high esteem. The Glorious Church appeared in China and <u>the gates of hell could not prevail against it</u>!

CHAPTER TWO,
The Ten Virgins

We believe in what is called the rapture of the church. The apostle Paul prophesied that in a twinkling of an eye we will be taken up! But the Lord also said, "One will be taken and one left." Jesus had a tremendous burden to convey to the whole church what the kingdom of God really is and on what basis we will be judged on the day of the Lord. He said in Luke 21:34 *"Watch ye therefore, and pray always, that you may you be accounted worthy to escape all these things that shall come to pass, and to stand before the Son of man."* <u>Like never before, this should be a byword today for all Christians</u>. We are living in perilous times. Sin is rampant without and within the church. While it should be getting ready for that glorious day when the Lord comes to take out his bride, the church is very busy with new programs, new buildings, even new doctrines (but not throwing out the false doctrines that have crept into Christianity) All of this in order to get bigger and more glorious in the sight of man, while forgetting about personal and corporate holiness, and most of all, losing that first love for the Lord Jesus Christ..

To illustrate the glorious church in good times and bad; if you observe a forest when all the trees are green, perhaps you will not notice a great difference between one kind of tree and another. But let's say that a disease affects all the trees except one kind and only that kind is left green. It would be very easy then to see which trees are the hardiest. In the same manner, when the world goes from bad to worse and some Christians do not change their values, but truly love their fellow man and serve the Lord, it would be very easy to see who is Christian, right?

Today in the whole world God is dividing the waters. Some Christians are being deceived by the world and saying, "But things are different now. Things have changed. People are smarter now. The church should keep up with the times. We've got to make the visitors comfortable when they come in." We must not scare them away. They will see what a good time we have and want to stay! Is that the gospel that Jesus wanted us to preach?

In Mathew chapters 24 and 25 Jesus gives a tremendously important discourse on the end of the age and warnings that we should be ready when he comes. He compares it to the time of Noah when only eight persons were saved and that none of the rest were ready. He also compares it to the destruction of Sodom when only Lot and his two daughters were saved, and they just barely! Then he gives four different illustrations of those that overcome and those that don't. The first example is of two <u>servants</u> (preachers) who had a ministry. One was faithful and one was not faithful. The faithful servant was accepted and the unfaithful servant was rejected. The second example is about Christians in general, the Ten Virgins. Some made it and some didn't. The third example of the talents is how we will be judged according to the capacity the Lord has given us. The last example is of those in the nations who were judged according to their compassion and work for their fellow man.

Let us consider the example of the ten virgins in Mathew 25:1-13. The Lord uses the Jewish wedding tradition and compares it to his coming for his beloved church, his bride. In that tradition the bridegroom proposes to his fiancée and she accepts, but they do not live together until *he has gone and prepared a place for them.* While he prepares a place, (his business, his farm, his house, all that they need to live and form a family) the bride keeps herself pure and prepares her dowry and the bridesmaids who will accompany her in the consummation of their marriage.

The parables or examples the Lord gave are to clarify our thinking and understanding by using common life examples. From this example we see that there were ten. All were virgins and all were waiting on the Lord to come after them. But only five were ready! The five that were not ready didn't have enough of their own oil. Oil depicts anointing. The anointing to speak the words of the Lord, to do the works of the Lord by his grace (undeserved power of the Lord). This grace can be described *as the life of Jesus flowing in and through us to do God's will on earth!* The servants of the Lord in the Old Testament were anointed for service, so oil depicts service also! Oil produces light and so does Christian service. We will be light for the world when we do the will of God for our lives. The five who were left behind depended on others for their oil (faith). Many are like that. They say, "Our church believes thus and so," or "Our pastor teaches this way." If someone is sick, they need for someone else to pray for them. In an emergency they look for all the human salvation first before they even think about praying. But what is most important, they do not have a personal relationship with the Lord! During meetings in the church, they are great Christians, but come Monday and you can not tell them from any unbeliever!

The Lord said to the five that came late, "I know you not! (Intimately) What a terrible indictment! How terrible to be left behind! Could it be that the Lord is condemning them to eternal damnation? I think not, though what has just happened to them is <u>very</u> serious. The Lord who is not willing that any should perish might give them another chance. We are dealing with reality here. (Wishful thinking will not change the Word) From that point on, from the moment that the Lord calls out his chosen ones to escape the wrath of God which will almost immediately begin to be poured out, there seems to be no true witness upon the earth for some time. There will be a time when no one around here will be proclaiming the Word of God. ((Revelation 8 through 12) No one will be encouraging the weak in faith. The apostate churches will be proclaiming their type of love, which in reality is self-love and licentious passion. Evil will very quickly be manifest in every area of life on the planet earth. There will be the homosexual churches. There will be the churches that preach peace with the sign of the upside down and broken cross. There will be churches that preach a freedom in love (which is not really love but passion. <u>Just Do It!</u>) There will be churches that preach riches (of this world). But there will be no one to encourage the desperate soul for whom Jesus came to give new life. *From the sound of the trumpet that calls the chosen ones to go up with Jesus until the Anti-Christ makes his move to take over the world, the saints do not appear in the Scripture.* No one is turning away from their idol worship, nor their murders, nor their sorceries, nor their fornication's, nor their thefts. (Rev, 9:20-21)

But low and behold, there are some (among whom may be of the virgins left behind) who decide that neither the filthy life nor the false teaching of the big preachers is for them and they remember that if anyone takes the mark of the beast in order to be accepted in the society and to buy or sell anything, they will be damned to hell. They decide in all this that they want to be with Jesus. At that point their salvation, perhaps the only salvation, is martyrdom. We read in Revelation 14:6-13 a completely different scenario than what we have today. The gospel is preached by three angels because the true church is now gone. Note that this gospel includes the warning of judgment! Then they say, "Blessed are the dead who die in the Lord from this time forth!" Some preachers use this at funerals to console those who have lost a loved one. There are other verses they could use that console the folks like "Blessed in the sight of the Lord is the death of his saints:" They are using a verse that is proclaiming a very important fact that Christians would do well to take into account. The fact is this; there will come a time after the glorious church has been taken up that the most blessed thing that could happen to you is that they cut off your head because you belong to Jesus and tell them so! The alternative would be to be condemned to hell! They will be killing everybody that says he belongs to Jesus! So perhaps Jesus has given the five rejected virgins a chance to be in a very special group in all eternity, the group of martyrs! (Rev, 12:13)

The parable of the TWO SERVANTS speaks of Ministers of the gospel. Those that have received the call and anointing to watch over the flock will receive a more severe judgment (Ja. 3:1) because (1) they know the will of their Lord, (2) they have received more power to overcome evil and (3) because they become responsible for the lives of many others. In Math.24:48-51 that evil servant who did not do the will of his master is thrown out with the hypocrites, (because he is one also). But the good and faithful servant was praised and accepted.

The parable of the TALENTS shows that Jesus will be just as pleased with the servant who had less ability but was faithful to do the best of his ability as with the servant with much ability. The "servants" represent all Christians in this parable. But the Christian who hid his talent was rejected. Those who hide their Christianity and do not serve the Lord fall in this group. Jesus called us all to be his witnesses in Acts 1:8 (for which we need the power of the Holy Spirit) and commanded us to preach the Gospel to every creature.

The parable of the judgment from the THRONE OF HIS GLORY. (Mt. 25:31-46) There are several opinions about who this group represents. It is obvious that the "goats" were not concerned about others who are hurting. The parable may include those many people in all ages that have <u>never heard nor understood the gospel.</u> Another understanding is that the goats represent church goers who don't have a personal relationship with the Lord and their lives show it. Sheep and goats are two types of animals which are very different in nature. Sheep are submissive. They like to be guided and led to green pastures. But they are not very smart (ouch!). They need leadership. Goats are very different. They are smart and independent. They can feign for themselves, but they are also very destructive. They soon destroy all the vegetation around where they are grazing. In Ro. 2:6, Paul spoke of "the righteous judgment of God, who will render to every man according to his deeds. To them who by patient continuance in well doing seek for glory and honor and immortality, and eternal life: but unto them that are contentious and do not obey the truth, but obey unrighteousness, indignation and wrath tribulation and anguish, upon every soul of man that doeth evil, to the Jew first and also to the Gentile, but glory honor and peace to *every one* that worketh good, to the Jew first and also to the Gentile." Those who had mercy and love for their fellow man were included and those who had no thought or compassion for their fellow man were excluded.

CHAPTER THREE
Jesus Christ's Message to the Seven Churches

Revelation is a prophetic book. The author, the apostle John, calls it a prophecy. From beginning to end it is loaded with symbols and types. John was "in the spirit on the Lord's Day" and the Lord himself appeared to him and gave him these seven messages to the seven churches in Asia. Prophecies throughout the Bible often have double edges, one for the time present and one for the future. Also, prophecies often use symbolic language that represent something larger or something in the future. These seven messages are like tha.t (chapters 2 and 3) There were seven living churches in Asia at the time of his writing and these messages were surely for them in that day. However, seven in the entire Bible is a symbol of fullness or completeness.

The Lord told him that the entire prophecy (The book of Revelation) was directed to the seven churches which would mean that the churches represent the entire church age. Again, he speaks, "The mystery of the seven stars which thou sawest in my right hand, and the seven golden candlesticks. The seven stars are the angels (messengers) of the seven churches; and the seven candlesticks are the seven churches." (Rev 1:20) We will study the messages from the viewpoint that the Lord's personal appearance in all his majesty to John and all these revelations were not just to seven local churches at that time, but to the entire church in all ages, the complete picture of the history of the church and the Lord's judgment of it. This will become self-evident.

The first three churches represent the period after the pioneer apostolic church. At that time the church was still considered to be one. So, Ephesus passed away before Smyrna appeared and Smyrna passed away before Pergamos appeared and Pergamos morphed into Thyatira. These three churches have all terminated because the Lord does not mention his return in his messages to them. But in each of the following messages, the Lord warns them to be ready when he comes, which indicates that each of these churches will be in existence when he comes to take out his bride which is that glorious church without spot or wrinkle. In the introduction of each message, the Lord tells something about himself, then his praise or criticism, or both, and then a special promise to those who overcome (remain steadfast in the faith) .

To EPHESUS he reminds us that he holds the seven stars in <u>his right hand</u>. The seven stars are the angel messengers to each of the seven churches and that he himself walks in the midst of the churches. The Lord is very much interested in the activities and growth of each church. When the Lord said, "I will build my church" it was based on the same confession that Peter made, "Thou art the Christ, the Son of the Living God" On that confession of that rock which is Christ himself, he would build his church. The Church is of God and it is of man. It has one foot on earth and one in heaven so to speak. It is important to understand that each local church is both human and divine, much the same way as a Christian who has the Spirit of Christ in him, yet he has to struggle with the flesh. Christ is in the midst of his churches and he is constantly by his Spirit wanting to guide his churches but the churches don't always listen. Though the first three church types have passed away, they leave us important lessons that we should learn. The lesson of the over comers in each church is for all of us. I believe that the overcomers will be taken up in the rapture along with the Philadelphia church which is the only church that has the specific promise of being "kept from the hour of temptation", or in other words, taken out. In this and all the seven messages, the Lord ends with "He that hath an ear, let him hear what the Spirit saith to the churches." Besides the written Word that he has left us, the Spirit of Christ and the Spirit of God are in the church to reprove and to guide us. Let us hear!

EPHESUS was a thriving and working church. It was large in number, encompassing the entire city of Ephesus. But in their busyness, they were neglecting the most important, their love relationship with the Lord. The Lord says that is not good. They had judged the false apostles, which was good, but there was something false creeping into their practice, the deeds of the *Nicolaitanes,* the "spiritual" ones lording it over the common people instead of helping them to have a personal walk with the Lord The Lord hates that! Religion can never replace a love relationship with the Lord! The promise to the over comers in Ephesus is that they may eat of the tree of life in the Paradise of God (The tree of life denotes eternal life. It disappeared in Genesis because sin is incompatible with eternal life and doesn't appear again until Revelation!)

SMYRNA is the suffering church. The most severe persecution against Christians in the Roman Empire came at that time. In Rome they were driven to live in the catacombs. They were tortured and killed. Some were burned alive, others fed to lions. The Lord had no criticism for them only to say that indeed they were rich (spiritually) and for them to hold on (to the faith)! And that their suffering would endure ten days. Figuratively meaning that there would be an end to their time of suffering. He promised the over comers that were faithful unto death, that they would not be hurt of the second death (condemnation). Although this church has disappeared, the severe persecution certainly has not! Some say that in the 20th century more Christians were killed for their faith than in all the other centuries put together! The mainstream press does not report to us many times when Christians are killed, even massacred in different parts of the world today.

PERGAMOS means marriage. Unfortunately, when the great persecution from Rome ended, the church was not prepared for the next trial that would come upon them which was power and riches. I wouldn't say prosperity because the soul of the church was not prospering. Constantine, the Roman emperor had just converted to Christianity. He saw a cross in the sky and heard the words, "by this sign shall you conquer" He declared the entire Roman Empire Christian, just like that!

One day they were pluralistic pagans, the next day they were all "Christians".

He marched the army into the river to be baptized! The pagan temples were turned over to Christians to use. The idea of the Christian temple became part of Christian doctrine because of this. The "clergy" received pay from the state. No more money problems! Since the pagans had suddenly become Christians, they were not spiritual and so the "clergy" had to tell them everything they could do and couldn't do. The deeds of the *Nicolaitanes* (power over the lay men or common people) became a <u>doctrine </u>which taught that there was a clergy (spiritual ones) and lay men (non-spiritual ones). The deeds that Jesus hates (in Ephesus) became the teaching that Jesus hates. An error of the church becomes a doctrine of the church if it is not corrected! So unfortunately, the church was "marrying" the state in an unholy matrimony.

Some of the elders warned of the great danger that lay ahead if they joined with the State but their cries were drowned out by the roll of money in the coffers! And the power! It was really heady, all the power of Rome backed up what the ministers decided! There is a promise to those that overcame, a new name that no one knows but he that receives it. Conversion to the Lord had become a very private thing. Men's doctrines began to be mixed with the Word of God.

THYATIRA means *sacrifice*. Text (Rev. 2:18-29) "And unto the angel of the church in Thyatira write "These things saith the Son of God, who hath his eyes like unto a flame of fire, and his feet are like fine brass. I know thy works, and charity and service, and faith, and thy patience, and the last works to be more that the first. Notwithstanding I have a few things against thee, because you suffer that woman Jezebel, which calls herself a prophetess, to teach and to seduce my servants to commit fornication, and to eat things sacrificed unto idols. And I gave her space to repent of her fornication and she repented not.

Behold, I will cast her into a bed, and them that commit adultery with her into great tribulation, except they repent of their deeds. And I will kill her children with death and all the churches shall know that I am he who searches the reins and hearts and I will give unto every one of you according two your works.

But unto you I say, and unto the rest in Thyatira, as many as have not this doctrine, and which have not known the depths of Satan, (as they speak), I will put upon you none other burden. But that which you have already, hold fast *till I come*. And he that overcomes, and keeps my works unto the end, to him will I give power over the nations *and he shall rule them with a rod of iron, as the vessels of a potter shall they be broken to shivers*: even as I received of my Father. And I will give him the morning star, He that hath and ear, let him hear what the Spirit says to the churches." (The promises to the over comers are also to all the over comers in all the churches.)

The church of Ephesus is passed, the church of Smyrna is passed and the church of Pergamos has evolved into Thyatira where the spirit of Jezebel is predominant. Jezebel was the daughter of the king of Phoenicia, a pagan king. She married Ahab, the king of Israel. Though Ahab was a bad actor, he was nothing compared to his wife. She brought idolatry into the culture of the people of God. That is what the Thyatira church is up to this day. Idolatry mixed with Christianity. It is interesting that the Lord describes himself with "eyes like a flame of fire and feet of brass". The aspect of a judge! His promise of judgment is severe for all her children (those that follow that Jezebel spirit). Spiritual fornication is unfaithfulness.

A "priest" can study seven years to learn the doctrines and ways of the "church", and still know very little about the Word of God. So, what can he teach his people unless he has a personal encounter with the Lord? Rev chapter 17shows us the final judgment of the great harlot. (Harlot of course being the extreme opposite of the virgin bride of Christ.)

But we see over comers in this church as well. The Lord says there are those that have not followed the Jezebel spirit (idolatry) nor tasted of the "deep things of Satan" (The many mysteries of that church.)

Early in my Christian experience the Lord taught me something very important. I was doing some carpentry work on a house under construction and the plumber came to do the rough in plumbing. We worked together from Monday to Friday. We would take a break together and I soon learned that he was a committed Christian. We had very good fellowship all week, but it wasn't till Friday that I discovered that he was a member of a church that we considered to be totally apostate. Had I known he belonged to that church on Monday, I may not have had all that good fellowship with my brother, but God was teaching me that he has dear children in many churches, not only those that we always approve of! He told me in his church, there are those that are of the faith and the others are political. There is also a tremendous promise to those that overcome in Thyatira, to rule over the nations with a rod of iron! He tells them to hold fast till he comes! That also means that this church will be around when the Lord comes back.

THE CHURCH IN SARDIS Text (Rev 3:1-6) "And unto the angel of the church in SARDIS write, These things saith he that hath the seven Spirits of God and the seven stars. I know thy works, that thou hast a name that thou livest, and art dead. Be watchful and strengthen those things which remain, that are ready to die: for I have not found thy works perfect (*perfected*) before God. Remember therefore how thou hast received and heard, and hold fast, and repent. If therefore thou shalt not watch, *I will come on thee as a thief,* and thou shalt not know what hour I will come upon thee. Thou hast a few names in even Sardis which have not defiled their garments and they shall walk with me in white for they are worthy. He that overcometh, the same shall be clothed in white raiment and I will not blot out his name out of the book of life, but I will confess his name before my Father, and before his angels. He that hath an ear, let him hear what the Spirit saith unto the churches."

Sardis is the church of the reformation. Sardis means *"Remnant"* When Martin Luther tacked his 95 thesis for debate on the door of the Castle Church in Wittenberg, he didn't realize it, but this would spark a spiritual revolution that would change the face of Christianity and when Christianity changed the entire world began to change! Light came into the world and light brought salvation and godliness. And all that brought human progress. Martin Luther was instrumental in all this. He ushered in a new way of looking at life in fellowship with God and our fellow man. But he wasn't the only one. Many others took up the torch of bringing the Word of God to the common man. Why then was the Lord's criticism of Sardis so severe? "You have a name that you are living but you are dead!"

The Reformation was time of rebirth and new life, but also a turbulent time with much violence and lack of love. Each one thought they had to eliminate those that didn't believe the same. In Europe there were 40 years of war between Christians. The Catholics burned those who didn't agree with them, and the Lutherans drowned the Anabaptists who believed that only believers should be baptized. In Geneva, the elders of the city under John Calvin hanged the dissenters that didn't agree with the official doctrine. And yet, in the midst of all this the *light* was appearing. Not everyone accepted it. But those that did accept new light thought they had it all. But meanwhile, there were men and women willing to face the wrath of Rome (and other Reform Churches) to stand on the truth that they saw. Martin Luther opened the way and many others followed, bringing in more light, Zwingli, Melanchthon, Menno Simons, then Calvin and Knox and many others. That light was what they saw, and it did change the history of the world as they walked in the light that they saw.

However, God will restore <u>all the truth</u> and all the glory of that first glorious church. But men camped around their particular revelation and around their man that brought it. So Luther's followers became Lutherans, and those that discovered the government in the church by the "presbytery" became Presbyterians, those that followed Menno Simons became Mennonites, those that saw baptism in water became Baptists! But Christianity is not a mere creed or confession, it's **the**

ultimate reality in Christ Jesus! It's Christ in us, the hope of glory! Neither did they endeavor to keep searching the Scripture to correct all the errors the marriage to the State, the pagan idolatry and the Jezebel spirit had brought into the Church! The meaning of the word perfect in Rev.3:2 is perfected or brought into perfection so that it would read, "I have not found your works *brought into perfection*". Since they were so proud of their doctrine and their great leader who had founded their doctrine, they sat upon that until it became only an empty shell. And their relationship with the Lord was being emptied out. Finally they only have a name that they are living but they are dead, says the Lord. Where do we stand before the Lord at this moment? Are we Sardis? Do we still have some of the Sardis spirit?

We must be very clear, however that we are not only talking about doctrine, though the truths of the Scriptures are very important and those truths are revealed to us by revelation, God is interested in life! Jesus said, "This is life eternal that they might know you, the only true God and Jesus Christ whom thou hast sent." God has given us his Word for the purpose of knowing him better and knowing his ways that we might walk in them, yet the simplest Christian that does not know much of the Word yet can still have a beautiful and glorious relationship with Jesus without yet knowing much Scripture. That is the trouble with Sardis. Their relationship with the Lord is dead. Notwithstanding, many times in the history especially in times of severe persecution, many churches have been transformed and the glorious church has appeared, washed of every spot and wrinkle. The purpose of all Scriptural revelation is that we might have a closer and purer relationship with our Lord Jesus. We can be cleansed and sanctified by the washing of the water by the Word (Eph. 5:26), which is by far the easiest way, or we can be purified by fire of severe trials. Also, the baptism in the Holy Spirit of God brings a cleansing fire, (Luke 3:16). We must pay attention to the Lord's dealing with us! (Our God is a consuming fire. Heb. 12:29) We don't really desire it, but severe persecution often brings that pure relationship into being. The Glorious Church appears when all else seems to be lost, all of man's ways come to an end, when there is no other way to turn, when all human and logical solutions fail. That's when the *Solid Rock* (Jesus) becomes the most beautiful thing in our lives!

The problem with the church of Sardis is that, though they admit that they have no power, they don't want to change. Their faith is in their doctrines even though some are man's interpretation more than a personal relationship with the Lord Jesus Christ. But the indictment of the Lord is terrible, *"You have a name that you are living but you are dead!"* Thank God there are some in Sardis who have not defiled their garments and they will walk with him in white!

Jesus said, "and this is the condemnation, that light has come into the world, and men loved darkness rather than light..." (Jn 3:19) The church we attended when we found the Way and began to walk with the Lord, was thriving with two services on the Sunday morning, one in the evening and prayer meeting on Thursday evening. On Sunday evening there was lots of singing and praise. I so much enjoyed them all. Sunday school and Vacation Bible school were well attended and successful. I taught young people's Sunday school class and enjoyed it very much. Besides the regular meetings, there were four young couples with little children who were very good friends and we would get together quite often, usually on Sunday afternoon and provoke each other to study the Bible more as we often had questions about the Word. It was a time of spiritual growth for us and many more. We ran out of room for Sunday school and had to build two temporary rooms to accommodate the classes and we were planning a large new church building.

But then we came to a crossroads in the Way and the Lord wanted to take us on. It was the year 1967, the year of the Israel's famous six-day war in which, though Jews were far outnumber by their attackers, they defeated all their enemies on every side in just six days! A tremendous miracle and fulfillment of prophecy as the Jews took back the other half of Jerusalem. (Read Zac 12) This was a prophetic time for the church as well. Jesus said that Jerusalem would fall into the hands of the gentiles until the time of the gentiles be fulfilled! Now Jerusalem again belonged to the Jews. The six-day war marked the beginning of the last generation "<u>which will not pass away until all things be fulfilled</u>." (Luke 21:20-33) At the same time, God began to pour out his Spirit on many people, on Episcopalians, Presbyterians, Baptists. (My wife and I received the baptism in the Holy Spirit with the gift of tongues in February of 1968) But the authorities of the church and many of the people rejected the move of God. Some of our dear friends also rejected it affirming that speaking in tongues was of the devil.

My family and I went to Colombia that year to serve as short term assistants with Wycliffe Bible Translators. When we came back to visit the church in 1972, the pastor pressured us not to speak in public about the baptism in the Holy Spirit. It was sad. They suggested that we leave the church, which we did. The Lord had called us to full time service and we planned to seek missionary training in the Midwest, so we just left quietly. But when we again visited the church many years later, they had never built the new building. There was no need for it. The congregation consisted of just a few families and the building was very much neglected and in disrepair. THE MOVE OF GOD HAD PASSED THEM BY.

THE CHURCH IN PHILADELPHIA. Philadelphia means brotherly love. In this church the brethren truly love one another as the Lord commanded. "By this shall all men know that you are my disciples if you have love one to another." Jn. 13:35

Text (Rev 3:7-13) "And to the angel of the church in Philadelphia write; These things saith he that is holy, he that is true, he that hath the key of David; He that openeth and no man shutteth, he that shutteth and no man openeth. I know thy works, behold. I have set before thee an open door, and no man can shut it; for thou hast a little strength, and hast kept my Word and hast not denied my name. Behold I will make them of the synagogue of Satan, which say they are Jews (God's people) , and are not, but do lie; behold, I will make them to come and worship before thy feet, and to know that I have loved thee. Because thou hast kept the word of my patience, I will also keep thee from the <u>hour of temptation,</u> which shall come upon the entire world, to try them that dwell upon the earth."

"Behold, I come quickly, hold that fast that no man take thy crown. Him that overcometh will I make a pillar in the temple of my God, and he shall go no more out, and I shall write upon him the name of my God, and the name of the city of my God, which is new Jerusalem, which cometh down out of heaven from my God: and I will write upon him my new name. He that hath and ear, let him hear what the Spirit saith unto the churches."

<u>This is the glorious church!</u> This is the church that Paul describes in Ephesians 5, without spot or wrinkle. This is the bride of Christ! God help us to desire with all our hearts to be a part of it! Twice he reminds us that this church will be taken up in the "Rapture"; that he will keep us from the hour of temptation which will come upon the entire world, and that he will make us part of the heavenly Jerusalem "which cometh down out of heaven" that we will be part of that great city which will govern the world for a thousand years!

Why is the Lord's message to Philadelphia so different than his messages to the other churches? It is no mystery when you carefully read what he said about this church. The plan and purpose of God, reiterated all through the Bible is to prepare a people for himself, *A people among which He feels comfortable to live.* God has a father's heart and wants to have many sons just like Jesus! We see in Philadelphia a people that really love one another. The apostle John said, "How can you say you love God whom you have not seen if you don't love your brother whom you have seen?" and "If we walk in the light as he is in the light, we have fellowship one with another and the blood of Jesus Christ his Son cleanses us from all sin." Fellowship is the translation of the word *koinoneo* which contains the following meanings; partnership, participation, social intercourse, benefaction, communication, distribution, all that is a lot more than a cold handshake after the meeting! Every born-again Christian has had a personal experience with our Lord and has dealt with (confesses) his past life and sins before the Lord. That is a very personal encounter without which I don't know how anyone can be sure they are saved.

Peter shouted, "You are the Christ, the son of the living God!" The Jews had long waited for and yearned for, the coming of the Messiah, the Christ, the anointed One. Paraklesis was the word they used which meant "the consolation of Israel", in other words "the Messiah!"(Lucas 2:25) Now Peter was talking to him face to face! Our relationship with Jesus and by him with our Father God must be very personal. When we pray in our "closet", we need to know who we are talking to. You can't just talk to the air for an hour. Perhaps that's why so many find it hard to pray more than five minutes at a time! But out of that very personal relationship must come a corporate relationship. We discover as we walk with the Lord that we are part of <u>*a body of people*</u> that God is putting together. A great part of our growth as disciples of the Lord is <u>learning to work together</u>, to share together, to love one another, and just plain learn how to function as part of a body, part of the developing bride of Christ!

In Philadelphia they read, study and <u>obey</u> his Word and are not ashamed to let it be known that they are Christians! To them the Bible is more important than tradition. When the Bible does not agree with tradition, they leave man's tradition behind and follow the Bible, no matter what men may say. They don't depend on a powerful organization but trust in the Lord for everything they do, they have to cry out to the Lord for help because they don't have the money to do it nor the wherewithal. The Lord is always giving them a job that is <u>far too big for them</u>! So they are encouraged to pray, nay they are pressed into prayer! Since their doctrine is the pure Word of God in the Bible, they may be criticized and even ostracized by other churches. For some reason they have little organizational power. They have to trust the Lord for their every need. God is their supply! Could it be that for these simple reasons they are the "chosen ones". My answer is of course it could be! Our God desires to have a people. He yearns to have a people. But they must love him with all their heart and all their soul and all their strength. And they must love their neighbor as themselves. It is so simple but it is so hard. And that is why many times the Glorious Church only appears in severe persecution or suffering. Their desires are purified because they are desperate. Now they haven't got time for petty gossip and besides they need one another. The persisting temptations drop away. Now the most beautiful and lovely thing is to be close to the Lord! But it doesn't have to be so only in severe situations. The Lord gave his life to set us free!

Isaiah proclaimed, "For though thy people Israel be as the sand of the sea, yet a remnant of them shall return; the consumption decreed shall *overflow* with <u>righteousness</u>." (Is 10:22) The apostle Paul spoke of the Israelites who were saved from slavery in Egypt by the mighty hand of God and tremendous miracles, such as we have not seen. Yet only a remnant was saved. Paul said, "But with many of them God was not well pleased: for they were overthrown in the wilderness." God only saved about one third of them, the ones under 20 years old plus Joshua and Caleb. But <u>all of them</u> had seen the mighty works of God and <u>all of them</u> were baptized in the sea and the cloud. (baptism in water and in the Holy Spirit) Moses was a special case because as God's prophet he struck the rock twice when God told him to speak to it. The precious picture God wanted to paint was Jesus who was crucified once for all our sins. Moses lost his chance to enter the Promised Land but was not condemned with the people.

The Philadelphia Church is the same church Paul describes in Ephesians 5:25-27, the church without spot or wrinkle or any such thing but is holy and without blemish. That is the church that he is preparing. That is the church that he loves. Should we even think of building a church that is less than this? Why were the Israelites overthrown in the wilderness? Hebrews 4:2 says that the word preached to them and the promises of God given to them did not profit them because it was not mixed with faith in them that heard it. Then the author adds an astounding pronouncement, <u>They will not enter in to my rest</u> *"although the works were finished from the foundation of the earth". (4;3b)* Their entering in to the Promised Land was guaranteed. They could not fail! God had ordained it and no man could change that,....except the people to whom the promise was made! But they cried out and blamed God and Moses and maybe even their luck. <u>Somebody</u> had to be to blame for this hard situation they found themselves in! They were afraid! The enemy is greater than us! We will all perish! Our children will perish! (Now they have found a sanctified reason not to face the enemy!) They wanted to protect their children! But in the end only their children that they wanted to protect were able to enter in to the Promised Land.

<u>But there were those who entered in</u>; Joshua and Caleb, who said, ***"If the Lord delight in us***, then he will bring us into this land, and give it (to) us, a land flowing with milk and honey!" (Num 14:8) So they and all those under 20 years old at the time of Israel's rebellion would represent the glorious church, and they took over the Promised Land!

And now as then, many churches and many Christians are not entering in to his rest, and will not be taken up in glory when he comes because they are not really obedient to his Word, they are not really loving him more that the rest. <u>They are not really willing to put him first</u>. They will be left behind, *even though the works were finished from the foundation of the world for them to enter in!* The key phrase is this; ***If the Lord delight in us***, he will take us with him.

LAODICEA means opinion of the lay people. Carnal believers base their opinions on what everyone else is doing and saying. (Rev 3:14-22)

"And unto the angel of the church of the Laodiceans write: These things saith the Amen, the faithful and true witness, the beginning of the creation of God: I know thy works that thou art <u>neither cold nor hot</u>. I would that thou wert either cold or hot, so because thou art lukewarm and neither cold nor hot, I will spew thee out of my mouth. Because thou sayest, I am rich and increased in goods and have need of nothing; and knowest not that thou art wretched, and miserable, and poor, and blind and naked. I counsel thee to buy of me gold tried in the fire, that thou mayest be rich, and white raiment that thou mayest be clothed, and that the shame of thy nakedness does not appear, and anoint thine eyes with eye salve that thou mayest see. Be zealous therefore, and repent. Behold, I stand at the door and knock, if any man hear my voice and open the door, I will come in to him and sup with him and he with me. To him that overcometh will I grant to sit with me in my throne, even as I also overcame and am set down with my Father in his throne. He that hath an ear let him hear what the Spirit saith unto the churches."

This church has lost its first love like the Ephesus Church. They have lost that personal relationship with the Lord. There is no fear of the God here. Ambitious to an extreme, they build huge "temples"! They are rich and have need of nothing! Their worship service is all sound and power, but its not the power of God, It's their own power. They have their preacher or preachers who are the spiritual ones (but the people will have their way!) He has to be very careful to give them what they want or they might leave (which they do quite often). "We need the numbers and we especially need those who have money, because we need lots of money to keep this thing going!" In some cases, their preacher is an idol where the whole movement depends on his dynamic personality.

The people have a mixed doctrine in their head, a little from the Bible, a little from what my grandmother taught me, a little from superstitions and a whole lot from this world's philosophy. They don't really know all the Word of God except the parts of verses that seem to promise God's blessing no matter what. And it's all okay because that's about the spiritual level of everybody else, so it must be alright!? (opinion of the laymen) The preacher is an organizer and entertainment expert. He organizes and gives them what they want. They have itching ears to hear some new doctrine that will make them feel good. **The (spiritual) service is a splendid show that could hold its own with anything Hollywood could do!** Money and politics are two driving forces in this church.

The mobile ministers demand x amount of money for their ministry if we want the privilege of their visit. But Jesus said, "Freely you have received, freely give." (Mt. 10:8) He also said, "A workman is worthy of his hire". So those who minister the Gospel can live by the Gospel, not get rich by the gospel. Can you imagine Peter saying, when they called him to pray for Dorcas, "you'll have to pay me so much for my ministry"? Paul said, "The children ought not to lay up for the parents, but the parents for the children." (2 Cor. 12:14) For the Laodiceans the proof that God is blessing a person's ministry is riches. "If they are rich, it's because God is blessing their ministry."

And finally, what is lukewarm? Is it not a mixture of hot and cold? They have great meetings on Sunday, the very best of everything. They are all lovely and well-dressed Christians, but come Monday at the workplace, on the street, in the school, they don't look or sound at all like Christians. Hot and cold are mixed! And it comes out lukewarm! They have a form of godliness, but deny the power thereof. And there is no fear of God! The terrible indictment of Jesus "I will spew them out of my mouth" The "gospel has deteriorated to: "This is who I am, this is how I feel, and <u>God is here to please me</u>" But the real gospel says: "This is who God is. This is how He feels, and <u>I am here to please God!</u>"

Laodicea doesn't have to be that way. The very reason for these prophecies is to wake people up that they might make ready for his coming. . There is a beautiful invitation and the best of promises for those in this type of church who have ears to listen. "I stand at the door and knock! If any man hear my voice and open the door, I will come in to him and sup with him and he with me!" (Notice that He is on the outside not on the inside) Then the best of promises, praise God, to the over comers "....I will grant to sit with me in my throne, even as I overcame and set with my Father on his throne.

In this message, the Lord says concerning his coming: "I am at the door!!" Could it be that this type of church is part of that great apostasy (falling away) that Paul warns us about?

CHAPTER FOUR
It is Finished!

Jesus had a tremendous job to do here on earth. Adam had really messed things up and Satan had seized control. All human help had failed. Adam had failed, Noah had failed to teach his sons, Abraham's sons were a mess and the people of Israel that God had ordained to usher in a better way of life had largely failed in what they were given to do. Then adding to the wrong, they opposed the prince of life when he came.

Someone had to right the wrongs and wrench the power from the hand of Satan. God would not do it, he was limited by his own ordinance that man was in charge of this world system! So Jesus took the long way around, but it was the only way. He started from scratch, as a baby, born of woman. He was the Son of God of course, but the Scripture says he put off his divinity and took the form of a servant, as man. (Phil. 2:6-8) He would live the entire life cycle as a man. He had to in every legal and moral sense of the word overcome sin, Satan and this world system. And he had to do it as a man. He was tempted in every point like as unto us, but without sin. (Heb. 4;15) He said, "Who can accuse me of sin?" (Jn 8:46) He had to overcome every kind of temptation, this world system and the devil. And he did it in broad daylight! He told the high priest, "I spoke openly to the world. I ever taught in the synagogue, and in the temple, whither the Jews always resort, and in secret I have said nothing. Ask the people I have taught. They will tell you what I said!" (Jn 18:20)

Satan himself could not stop him, or make him fall, though he tried. Oh how he tried! But Jesus *bound the strong man and spoiled his house!* (Mt 12:29, Mc 3:27) Jesus had overcome in every sense of the word, from childhood, through adolescence and manhood. He knew thirst, weariness, heat and cold, frustrating circumstances, and all without sin! But the worst was yet to come, HE HAD TO SUFFER FOR <u>OUR</u> SINS.

His disciples couldn't grasp it. They were sure he was the long-awaited Messiah, the anointed One, the Son of David, he who would restore Israel to her proper place in the world! Some things the human mind refuses to acknowledge if it's too far out from our scheme of things or would change something we hold on to very dearly. Jesus had told his disciples <u>seven</u> times that he had to suffer and die and be raised again. Yet when the time came, when the Jews took him prisoner, they were sure he would rise up and take over the kingdom of Israel and establish David's throne.

But Jesus had to suffer for our sins and for our full redemption. <u>His time in the garden of Gethsemane was crucial</u>. That is where the real battle took place. He came face to face with Satan and all the demons. Besides, he had to overcome every human desire to escape this terrible torture and death that was waiting for him. His agony was so great that his sweat was like great drops of blood! Perhaps he prayed for hours. His disciples slept, though he woke some of them up more than once. <u>He was alone</u>. There was no human help or comfort for him. Angels came and ministered to him. *but the battle was won in Gethsemane*! He stood up and returned to his disciples. He was ready! No Joshua was ever so brave! No Moses was ever more powerful! When the guards came to take him prisoner, as if he were a dangerous criminal, he stepped forward and said, "*I am he.* Let these go their way." When he said, I am **HE** (the great I AM) the guards fell back from the power coming out of him. Judas was there, the disciple who betrayed him, guiding the guards to where he knew Jesus would be. He too had believed that Jesus would take over the kingdom of Israel. But his belief had become an ideology, drowning out all reason, willing to lie and cheat and steal to make his belief a reality. His treason was so complete; he even kissed Jesus to identify him.

They bound Jesus and took him away, to be interrogated, beaten and insulted all through the night in a clandestine and mock trial. In the morning they took him to Pilate, the Roman governor who wanted nothing to do with him, but after the fashion of the Romans, had him bound to a post and flogged. The Romans were experts in torture and cruelty. Much has been said about the famous cat of nine tails which they used to scourge a prisoner. But though men died at times under the Roman scourge as it was called, the purpose of it was not to kill the person but to bring him to confess his crime, forty stripes, one by one. Even the bravest of men would cry and scream! Jesus did not confess of course. He had done nothing wrong. He didn't even cry out. The man (or men) who beat him must have been amazed! He took <u>our</u> stripes that were due unto us, for our sins and disobedience. But by his stripes are we healed! Both physically and spiritually!

Then they put a purple robe on his back. It would stick to the blood like glue, then they ripped it off and put it back on again, increasing the agony. They made a crown out of a thorn bush. If it was like the mesquite, it can have thorns up to two inches long. These would be deflected by the skull and slide down under the skin. Then they hit him on the head with a stick which would jam the thorns down further. They spate in his face and pulled out his beard. After Adam sinned, he was condemned to struggle with thorns and thistles; (the curse of Adam). Also, the Jews were warned if they didn't obey the law, they would be the scourge of the earth; (the curse of the law). Jesus took both curses on his body. He became a curse for us, that we might be redeemed from both curses. That we might be the head and not the tail. (Deut 28:13) That whatsoever we do might prosper! (Psalm 1:3)

Then they took him to Golgotha and nailed him to the cross. *Our Lord was nailed to the cross*! Again, we can be amazed at the expertise of the Romans. The nails had to be big enough to hold his weight, but had to pass through the flesh between the bones without breaking a major blood vessel which would make the prisoner bleed to death in a matter of minutes. They wanted him to hang on the cross and suffer. So, one man would steady the nail on his wrist or hand the other with a sledge hammer would drive it through the flesh and into the wood on the other side. Whether the feet were nailed with one nail or two the

Scripture does not say. If it was one nail, it would have to be a huge one, long enough to go through both feet and penetrate deeply into the wood below. In all that excruciating pain Jesus did not cry out. He was a lamb. <u>OUR SINS</u> WERE NAILED TO THE CROSS WITH JESUS. *he became sin for us!* And in that most terrible agony as Jesus was hanging on the cross, he said, "Father, ...*forgive them*.... They know not what they do!" **If that is not grace, the sky is not blue!**

Jesus hung on the cross covered with sin. It was so terrible that even the Father turned his face away. (The pain of our Father God was even greater to have to turn away from his Son!) That's when Jesus cried out, "My God, my God, <u>why</u> hast thou forsaken me? But there was a fire burning away that black sin. That fire was the pure virtue of a totally righteous man! He was a perfect man, the only perfect man. And then, as a perfect man he suffered for us, for our sins. For our naughtiness and our rebellions he was whipped at the stake, for our disobedience he suffered the crown of thorns and the disgrace. Our sins were nailed on the cross with Jesus! When that virtue had burned away all the dross and power of sin, it was consumed! He had finished the work! He had done <u>all the will of God for man from his birth until his trial.</u> He had drunk <u>the last drop from the bitter cup!</u> When it was consumed, he said, **IT IS FINISHED!** But as his virtue burned away the sin his very life was consumed....**And then he died.** <u>The skies were dark and angry and the very earth shook in a terrible earthquake.</u> The Roman Centurion and his guards, men hardened in the Roman culture and by their duties of cruelty were deeply touched, seeing that God himself had reacted in the darkened sky and the earthquake, exclaimed, "Truly this was the Son of God!" By comparison the religious figures of the day, steeped in their own self-righteousness and their ideology, even though they could see plainly that Jesus had fulfilled all prophecy, were unable to repent and glorify God! The veil of the temple in Jerusalem was rent from the top to the bottom, signifying that he had opened the *way* into the very presence of our Holy God! People must have been screaming in terror as the earth shook! Later two friends came and took his body down from the cross and took it away and laid it in a tomb, and then——there was only, *silence*.

For his disciples and all the people who believed in him this was a terrible time. All their hopes seemed to be dashed. This thing just gotten out of hand! They may have thought that at any moment Jesus would assert his power. But it kept going from bad to worse! And now he is dead! "They told us his body is in a grave somewhere!?"

It will help us to understand what Peter went through and why! Peter was a strong man, a leader among men. He was the "take charge" kind of a guy. He was many times the spokesman for the other men, speaking at times what they all felt. Though Peter's downfall was great when he denied the Lord, they all deserted the Lord in the moment he most needed support. But Peter's denial was so obvious. He had emphatically voiced his undying loyalty to the end, even if he had to die for the Lord! He was serious and would have carried through in the heat of battle. In the garden he raised a sword and struck the guard, cutting off his ear, and would have continued to fight, full of adrenaline. But the Lord told him to put away his sword; it was not time for that!

Peter was miffed to say the least. Confused and upset, Luke said he followed the troop that took Jesus prisoner, but *"afar off."* (Luke 22:54) He was pouting! He then entered the court yard of the high priest, and even began to warm himself at the fire of the adversaries. A girl accused him of being one of Jesus group. Big man Peter couldn't appear to be one of Jesus motley crew in front of this girl! Now his confusion gives way to fear. Big man Peter is afraid! Things are looking pretty bad for Jesus and all those who were with him. He says, "Woman, I know him not!" Peter is in a quandary, controlled by his flesh. Again, someone accuses him and he denies even knowing the Lord.———Somewhere out in the darkness a rooster crows.

About an hour later a man says, "<u>Yes you are</u> one of them, you even talk like them!" The Scripture says that for the third time Peter denies the Lord and even begins to curse and swear! At that moment Jesus from above in the palace looks down into the courtyard and as their eyes meet, a rooster crows again! Suddenly Peter is shocked with shame! He went outside and wept bitterly, feeling like an utter failure! He had a hard lesson to learn, that his earnest willingness to suffer and even die for Jesus was still in the strength of the flesh, earnest as it might seem. He had to learn that the flesh cannot be trusted. So now he was in self condemnation, sadness and despair. He, the brave one had committed the "unpardonable sin"!? Was he any better than Judas? The disciples thought all was lost. For three days and three nights they were all huddled together in their place, <u>having lost all hope.</u>

The Lamb of God, "He took on himself the form of a servant and was made in the likeness of men and...he humbled himself and became obedient unto death even the death of the cross. Wherefore God also hath highly exalted him, and given him a name which is above every name; that at the name of **Jesus** every knee should bow..... and every tongue should confess that <u>Jesus Christ is Lord</u> to the glory of God the Father." (Phil. 2:7-11)

A MIGHTY EARTHQUAKE CONVULSES THE EARTH! AN ANGEL OF GOD ROLLS BACK THE STONE! The Roman guards, mighty men of valor, quake and fear and faint away, their might and valor is useless to stop any of this!

GLORY TO GOD! The Lamb of God has now become *the* ***LION OF JUDAH***! In the early morning light he stands outside the grave, ***LORD OF ALL LORDS AND KING OF ALL KINGS!***. Neither man nor devil could stop him from doing all the will of God. <u>There is no power in heaven or on earth that can stop him now!</u> "OF

THE INCREASE OF HIS GOVERNMENT AND PEACE <u>THERE SHALL BE NO END</u>, UPON THE THRONE OF DAVID AND UPON HIS KINGDOM, TO ORDER IT AND TO ESTABLISH IT WITH JUSTICE AND WITH JUDGMENT FROM HENCEFORTH EVEN FOR EVER." (Is. 9:7) (like the reign of David but over all the eternal kingdom of God) But that's not all. He will ascend into heaven and come back in Spirit to inhabit each one of his children. Jesus in us and God in Jesus! The same power that raised Christ from the dead, <u>lives in his people</u>. (Eph 1:19-21)

That glorious morning when the angel appeared to Mary, he brought a message from the Risen Lord to his disciples and a special message for Peter. And here many of us can identify with Peter. The angel said, "Tell his disciples, <u>and Peter</u>...."

But now! The resurrected Jesus had sent Peter a personal message through the angel. When Mary brought that message and that he had said, *and Peter*, he must have cried out, "Is he *alive*? And did he say—Peter? Are you sure he said *Peter*?" And to himself, "I can't believe it! Does he still want to see me? Would he forgive me? I feel so unworthy! God would forgive me? Can all this be true?" Is he really alive?

Jesus must have had a private meeting with Peter, one of forgiveness and reconciliation. One so intimate that only they know what was said! We must not miss the lesson here. We now know how that later the Spirit-filled Peter was completely fearless before the fearsome Sanhedrin, knowing full well how they had orchestrated the death of Jesus and that they had prohibited the name of Jesus even be mentioned. But <u>filled with the Holy Ghost</u>, he said, "You rulers of the people, and elders of Israel, if this day we be examined of the good deed done to this impotent man (that had been miraculously healed), by what means he is made whole; **be it made known unto you all,** and to all the people of Israel, that by the name of **Jesus Christ of Nazareth**, whom <u>you crucified</u>, whom

God raised from the dead, even by him does this man stand before you whole. THIS IS THE STONE THAT WAS SET AT NOUGHT BY YOU BUILDERS WHICH HAS BECOME THE HEAD OF THE CORNER. Neither is there salvation in any other! for <u>there is no other name under heaven given unto men whereby we must be saved!</u>" (Acts 4:8-12) What made the tremendous transformation of Peter? ***The living Jesus was living in him!***

Not only was he fearless, he had the whole message of God in a moment! And this is what happened to Peter, "That is the mystery hidden in ages past but now is manifest to his saints, ...***which is Christ in you the hope of glory!***" (Col 1:27) Peter had to be emptied of self, he had to know as Paul proclaimed, for I know that in me (that is in my flesh) dwells no good thing! (Ro 7:18). But in Peter's deep self condemnation, he also had to learn of the mercy of God in Christ Jesus. Jesus <u>paid</u> for our sins. When he said, "**It is finished**!" It was all done. He had paid the price and what a tremendous price it was! Peter had to learn that, and <u>we have to learn that.</u> It's by mercy that we are saved. We are like one beggar showing another beggar where to get bread!

<u>*So those who have seen that go forth*</u>, not as one beating the air or running off in all directions or inventing ways to show how much faith they have, but as a bond servant waiting for the command of his master. They do nothing by impulse or for vainglory but say as Jesus said when he came into the world, "You have given me a body, I come oh Lord <u>to do your will</u>!" (Heb 10:6-7) And even the youths shall faint and be weary, and the young men shall utterly fall, <u>but they that wait upon the Lord</u> will renew their strength. They shall mount with wings as the eagles. They shall run and not be weary. They shall walk and not faint! (Is, 40:30-31)

CHAPTER FIVE
The Tabernacle of David

"WHOSO OFFERETH PRAISE GLORIFIETH ME

And to him that ordereth his conversation aright will I show the salvation of God!" (Ps 50:23) Where does this desire to praise God come from? It comes from deep within; the Spirit of Christ within us; the pure joy of knowing him, the King of all kings! Our Savior and Lord, our Sovereign, our Sanctifier, our Friend and Confidant! The more we know him the more we want to praise him and the more we praise him the more we love him! To praise God is the most repeated exhortation and commandment in the Bible.

David was a man after God's own heart and David's life was marked by praise from his time as a boy with his sheep in the lonely hills of Bethlehem until his final prayer of thanksgiving before he died. (1 Chr 29:10) Many of the Psalms of praise were written by him. The Children of Israel used the Psalms a hymn book.

God's promise for the new church was that he **would build again the tabernacle of David.** (Acts 15:16-17 taken from Amos 9:11) What was so special about the tabernacle of David that it would become a model for the Church of Jesus Christ? It was really just a tent with the ark of the covenant inside and musicians, Asaph and his brethren in charge of playing and singing praise to the Lord, day and night! And Zadok the high priest was to offer burnt offerings before the Presence of the Lord according to the law of Moses. David wrote a special Psalm for the musicians to sing, the key verse (1Chr 16:29) reads: "Give unto the Lord the glory due his name: bring and offering and come before the Lord in the beauty of holiness".(He copied it from Deut. 15:14)

The first thing we note about the tabernacle of David is its <u>simplicity</u>. It was a tent set up to guard the ark which represents <u>the presence of the Lord</u>. Before the Lord they worshipped and praised and offered burnt offerings day and night. That is the church! The Lord is in their midst! They worship him and praise him continually; by their lives (in the beauty of holiness) by their song of praise, by their thanksgiving coming truly from grateful hearts. David had a small amount of Scripture compared to us, but he wanted to fulfill all the Word of God.

So must be the Glorious Church. Simplicity, we have a Savior that loves us and wants to share our lives with us. It's all about real life, not religion! We are so thankful that he saved us and that every day we see his hand of mercy in our lives. The Tabernacle of David: 1) THE PRESENCE OF JESUS, 2) PRAISE AND WORSHIP and 3) OBEDIENCE TO THE WORD and the result is LIVES TRANSFORMED.

But Jesus said to wait. Wait for what? And who should wait? *There is an anointing for those who are willing to wait*! But not just to wait but to seek with all your heart! "Blessed are they which do hunger and thirst after righteousness for they shall be filled!" (Mt. 5:6) When we see the power and anointing that the first Christians had and we believe the Word of God our reaction should be,—"where is this power? I want all the power of God, once given to the early Christians!" In reality, what we need is more of Jesus, our resurrected Lord. He has all authority in heaven and earth! He is the source of all the power of God! When you get to the place that you want the fullness of his Holy Spirit more than anything else, you will receive it! In Luke 11:5 in answer to the disciples request to teach them to pray, Jesus gives the parable of the persistent friend who wouldn't take no for an answer. We need to get that desperate before the Lord. He only wants to purify our desires. But he promises that God will give the Holy Spirit to those that ask him.

The Navy Seals have won for themselves a special fame because of their courage and ability to rescue people in dangerous situations. It is no casual thing that they have earned this name because it goes back to the time when they were recruited. The Navy extends the invitation to all their servicemen but they make no bones about it. The training will be very hard and their eventual service as well. They must be willing to undergo the most rigorous training, even to the extreme limit of their physical and mental capabilities. Besides, they must realize that once they have completed a special mission, it is not for them to "sit on their laurels" or to bask in the fame, but to go on to further service for their country and for others.

In much the same way the Lord invites us to be his disciples. But he makes no bones about how easy it's going to be. He said, "if you don't give up your old life, your self-centered life, your life in the flesh, you cannot be my disciple." And it doesn't stop there. This is the real thing! He said, If they persecuted me, they will persecute you. If the world hated me it will hate you. There is a sense in which we must pass through the same types of things that he passed through. There will be a time when you feel all alone. Nobody seems to care or want to be with you. "If they hated me they will hate you!" But he also promised, "Blessed are you when all men speak evil of you <u>for my sake</u>! Blessed are you when men shall revile you and persecute you, and say all manner of evil against you falsely <u>for my sake</u>. Rejoice and be exceedingly glad: for great is your reward in heaven: for so persecuted they the prophets which were before you." (Mt 5:11-12) But we also have the promise that "He will not suffer you to be tempted above what you are able, but with the temptation will also make a way to escape that you may be able to bear it." (1Cor 10:13)

Do not settle for anything less. The Lord has a very special and exciting plan for your life.

YE SHALL RECEIVE POWER. In the midst of his practical teaching Paul reminds us of the secret to receive the power to overcome. "And be not drunk with wine wherein is excess *but be filled* with the Spirit" (Eph. 5:18). <u>That power that Jesus promised</u> (Acts 1:8) is first of all the power to live the resurrection life.

The resurrection life is the life on the other side of <u>death to self</u>, and risen anew, <u>*filled*</u> with the Spirit. Jesus promised the disciples that they would be *baptized* in the Holy Spirit and power. (Acts 1:5 & 8).

If that promise was only for his disciples at that moment as some say, then this author has been living a life of fantasy for the last 50 years since receiving that baptism in the Holy Spirit, and all the miracles of God that we've seen are only mirages. Read the rest of the book of Acts! It's full of records of dramatically changed lives and the power of God. That's the way the early church turned the world upside down! The entire Bible is the story of God working with man and how man had to <u>respond to God and humbly let God use him</u>. Jesus said, "If you then, being evil know how to give good gifts to your children, how much more shall your Heavenly Father give the <u>Holy Spirit</u> to them that ask him?" (Luke 11:13)

Baptism was not originally an English word. In the translating, the Greek word baptizò was directly transferred, or *transliterated* into the English New Testament. It was used to describe the process of dying cloth. It was *submerged to be changed*. When we are baptized in water, (submerged in water) by faith we are translated into the Kingdom of his dear Son. When we are <u>submerged</u> (baptized) in the Spirit of God, we are submerged in his Spirit and we have access to <u>another dimension</u> in our relationship with God and our Lord Jesus Christ. ACCESS is a key word. It is not our power but <u>access</u> to the power of God in our lives. It's not our holiness but access to the power to live a holy life. It's also like a private phone line to God.

When we get a glimpse of his <u>majesty</u>, of his <u>holiness</u>, of his <u>glory</u>, we cannot but praise and worship him. Then the gifts of the Spirit are made available to us, given as we hunger and thirst for more of God. God answers the heart cry and gives gifts to each according to his purpose in the life of each one. The manifestation of the `power of God will increase in these later times even more as sin increases in the world. If you are content to have a comfortable, mediocre Christianity, this will never happen to you.

It isn't for us to decide what we shall pass through, whether it will be hard or easy, whether there will be persecution or not. However, the apostle Paul warns us that "All who will live godly in Christ Jesus shall suffer persecution." And Jesus said "Blessed are you when all men speak evil of you. Great is your reward in heaven!" (Mt 5) No one particularly wants to suffer. And we should not seek persecution. What we should seek is to love God with all our hearts and our neighbor as our self.

The Lord has given us two models of the <u>glorious church</u>, the book of Ephesians, especially 5:22-33 and Revelation 3:7-13 and both speak of the same church. In Ephesians 5, Paul teaches about marriage, using that relationship to teach about the church and that is so very fitting because the glorious church, (the one which will be taken up in the rapture) will be his bride! God wants to build his Glorious Church composed of beautiful families (and singles too of course). The man is the head of the wife; Christ is the head of the church. He is Lord and sovereign over the church. If he is not Lord of all, he is not Lord at all (for us). This is fundamental if we desire to be that church without spot or wrinkle or any such thing, that gloriously beautiful bride waiting for her bridegroom!

Jesus said, "Because you have kept the Word of my patience (patiently kept my Word), I will keep you from the <u>hour of temptation</u> that will come upon the entire world to try them that dwell upon the earth." (Rev, 3:10) "There will come a time when they will not endure sound doctrine but will heap to themselves teachers having itching ears and they shall turn away their ears from the truth and shall be turned away unto fables." (2 Tim 4:3-4) Today in 2022, if any church will really hold their values and preach the full and true Gospel they might suffer persecution, some of which might come from other churches! If the parents would refuse to let their children be indoctrinated with sexual education, re-orientation about families, children choosing their sex, evolution, and the socialistic garbage, they might find themselves in a court of law. We are called to be LIGHT and SALT in this world, light *shining out of the darkness!* (2 Cor 4:6)

Light overcomes darkness. It doesn't fight darkness, it overcomes it! Everyone born of the Spirit is like the wind which when it meets an obstacle just goes around it but doesn't stop. But wind moves things. Like the wind, no one knows where the power comes from, but no one will deny that there is a wind blowing! And people will know when the power is truly flowing!

The Glorious Church is _Jesus in this world_. The Glorious Church is the <u>voice of prophecy in the world,</u> warning people of the wrath of God to come. The Glorious Church (while it is still here) <u>holds back the evil</u> in the world. Some say, but it's prophesied that things will go from bad to worse. It is also prophesied that we are light and salt! Also, "there is that which withholds" (The Spirit of God in the Church) and when the Glorious Church shall be taken out of the way, the evil one shall be revealed, "even him whose coming is after the work of Satan, with all power and signs and lying wonders, and with all deceitfulness of unrighteousness in them that perish: _because they received not the love of the truth that they might be saved._ And for this cause God shall send them STRONG DELUSION, <u>that they should believe a lie</u>. That they might be damned who believed not the truth, but had pleasure in unrighteousness." (2 Thes 2:9-12)

Amid all the unrighteousness and darkness that is coming over this world there is a <u>bright light</u>, and that bright light is the Glorious Church, pure and true to the Word of God. They don't have a special church doctrine because the Word of God is their doctrine. No one pretends to know it all but they agree that to the best of their knowledge and understanding they will believe and obey the Word. They have given up their high places (doctrines and traditions of man). They have decided to put the Kingdom of God and it's righteousness first as Jesus commanded. But more than anything else, **these people know the Lord**. He walks with them and leads them and calls them by name. From the least to the greatest of them, they all know him. He is among them and in them. (Eph 2:20-22) His love is flowing among them that no one be left behind.

And <u>they know his Word</u>. The pure Word of God is meat and drink for these people. The call of the world grows dim as they feed on his Word and each week he shows them new things in the Word, then during the week it works out in their lives. They understand what is happening in the world in the light of his Word.

Does all that sound like a beautiful tale but not reality? It should be our high calling of God in Christ Jesus! Our local church hasn't gotten there yet, but we are pressing on! Otherwise, do we have to wait for severe persecution to straighten out the church? Do we dare teach anything less? Hebrews 8:10 says *"For this is the covenant that I will make with the house of Israel after those days saith the Lord I will put my laws into their mind, and write them in their hearts, and I will be to them a God and they shall be to me a people.....for they shall all know me from the least to the greatest!"*

THE HIGH CALLING OF GOD IN CHRIST JESUS
That hope of glory is in your breast,
That you might know him even better than the rest.
The high calling of God, the way of the cross
You'll make the goal, no matter the cost!
But low and behold, this world drags you down
The flesh and the devil, there is nothing sound!
But you are the victor, it's in the Word!
You'll win and conquer, by the use of the "Sword"!
Your dreams are high for that noble prize
And you're very sure that this is right!
But if your dreams are dashed, the work and words of fools,
Can you stoop and build with worn out tools?
Can you lose, and start again at your beginnings
And never blame the others for your loss?
Can you force your heart and nerve and sinew
To serve the Lord long after "they" are gone?
Can you keep on going with all that is in you?

When all you can think to say is "hold on!"
The Lord is working in you to will and to do
And in his good pleasure you'll be made anew
You can talk to crowds and keep your virtue
And walk with kings—-nor lose the common touch,
Now neither foes nor loving friends can hurt you
And all men count but none too much
If you can fill that unforgiving minute
With sixty seconds of loving distance run
If you are known by your love and your truth,
One day you'll look for your enemies and there'll be none!
For Christ will come to you e'er the light is dim
He'll be your hope of glory! One day you'll be like him!

WHAT ARE THE HIGH PLACES?

The nation of Israel had high places that were not pleasing to the Lord. These were from idol worship or demon worship which the Israelites learned from the pagan people around them. Some of these practices were downright horrible, like offering their first born to a pagan god. Some children were even thrown in to fire and burned alive.

The people built niches or miniature temples to worship idols or demons, usually under a green tree on a high hill, perhaps because of this came the name "high place" Some of these places held a "high" place in the hearts of the people even after they turned back to God. Perhaps they had memories of the family visiting a place on a high hill and feeling good about it. They said, "We used to worship demons there but now we worship God there. We've dedicated that to God, so it's alright!? Of course Christians don't have any high places today! Or do they?

The high places became a stumbling block to the Jews even after they turned back to God. Joash, king of Judah and his son Amaziah (2 Kings 12 and 14), both did that which was right in the sight of the Lord, but the high places held the kingdom back from being all that God wanted it to be. Jesus said, "That which is born of the flesh is flesh and that which is born of the Spirit is spirit.! (Jn.3:6) That is a very important principle. Some of our "Christian" traditions were taken from pagan demon worship! Calling them "Christian" does not make them pleasing to God! 2 Kings 1:3 says "But the high places were not taken away. The people still sacrificed and burnt incense in the high places." If the Bible truly is as we confess, our guide in all things concerning faith and conduct, then we should ask ourselves concerning all our practices and doctrines, Is it Biblical? Did this practice have it's origin in demon worship? Knowing that, can I still say I do this in the name of Jesus?

LITTLE FOXES SPOIL THE VINES. "Catch for us the foxes, the little foxes that spoil the vines, for the vines have tender grapes." (Song 2:15) and "...exhort one another daily while it is called to day: lest any of you be hardened through the deceitfulness of sin:" (Heb 3:13) Sin creeps in, and sin is deceitful. (Heb 3:13) We need to learn to call sin by its name and not cover it up. And this goes for all Christians, great and small, old and young. Sin is easy to deal with in its beginnings, but it gets harder and harder as we allow it to take root. (James 1:12-15) We ourselves can be deceived by small sins and think, "it's not so bad!" That is why we are exhorted to confess our faults one to another and pray for one another. (James 5:16) Besides the daily review, the Lord has given us several occasions to examine ourselves. 1) When we are going to pray for a sick person (Ja 5) and 2) When we see a problem in our brother's life (Mt 7:3-5) and 3) before we partake of the Lord's Supper (1Cor 11:31) The New Testament has much to say to born again Christians about dealing with sin, and the reason is that though we have the Spirit of Christ within us, God in his wisdom has allowed us to keep living with the natural man so that now we have the Spirit of Christ but in our soul we have the old man. In all this our will is what makes the difference because he has given our will a certain amount of sovereignty. God will support us when we really decide we want to be free of sin. It is up to us to learn to submit our will to the Spirit of Christ within us which is one with our spirit. What a marvel! (1 -Cor 6:17 & Luke 18:2-14)

1Peter 1:15 says, "But as he which has called you is holy so be ye holy in all manner of conversation." And in the next chapter, points out a number of sins which we must learn to put away. In chapter 2:15, "<u>For so is the will of God</u>, that with well doing ye may put to silence the ignorance of foolish men." The apostle John throughout his first epistle tells us how to deal with sin and how to overcome this world system! Paul in the latter part of Ephesians teaches us how to deal with the world and the flesh as Christians.

CHRISTIAN TEMPLES. When Jesus said, "Destroy this temple (in Jerusalem) and in three days I will raise it up." (Jn 2:19 & 21) "he spake of the temple of his body." Even John and the other disciples probably didn't realize the full significance of what he was saying, because God was about to *change his relationship and point of contact with man.* Under the law of Moses, man was taught to fear a Holy God, and rightly so because sinners would be consumed before the mighty holy God if presented in their sin. The design of the temple and the order of worship were all designed to impress upon man that sin had put a <u>great distance between them</u>. The people were to go out and live their lives and do their work diligently and on the Sabbath come to the synagogue and worship, and at least three times a year they were to go to Jerusalem, to the temple and present a sacrifice for their sins in order to be allowed into the Holy place, But <u>the presence of God</u> was still far from them. It was separated behind the heavy veil which closed off the way into the Holy of Holies. The ark and the mercy seat hidden behind the veil represented our Lord Jesus. The ark contained three things; the tables of the law (only Jesus kept all the law), the urn with manna inside (Jesus is the bread from heaven), and the rod of Aaron that budded and Indicated that Aaron was God's high priest. Now Jesus is the high priest. So the Ark and the mercy seat above it in every sense represented our Lord Jesus. But the way into the holy of holies (the presence of God) was not open because Jesus had not yet shed his blood for us,.... not yet. But when Jesus died on the cross after saying **"It is finished!"** the veil was rent from top to the bottom, signifying that the way was open into the very presence of God because of the reconciliation made by his Christ, our Lord!

Then God destroyed the temple made of stones, not a stone was left unturned, and with it, the <u>system</u> of the temple worship was destroyed. God realized that the temple could also become a type of idolatry. Stephan saw it and prophetically declared that God does not dwell in temples made by human hands but in his new temple which is the body of Christ, the church. (Acts 6 &7 esp. 7:48-49) They stoned him for his prophetic words.

The first Christians saw it. They began to meet together, not only in the temple but from house to house. After they had to leave Jerusalem because of the persecution, they met together wherever they could, but we find no example of Christian "temples" in the New Testament. God wants us to return to the simplicity and purity of the Tabernacle of David. The <u>Presence of Jesus</u>, a <u>life of praise</u>, <u>obedience to the Word</u>. It isn't important where we meet, it can be a cave or a palace. We are the Body of Christ that was raised up after three days. (Jn. 2: 19-21)

CHAPTER SIX
The Marvelous Living Church!

Jesus said, "where (even) two or three are gathered in my name, there am I in the midst of them". <u>This is the "church which is his body, *the fullness of him that fills all things.*"</u> (Eph 1:22)

THE CHURCH IN A PRISON

A fighter pilot was downed in North Vietnam. He was taken captive by the Communists. The prison where he and many other prisoners of were housed was a large U-shaped affair, the cells forming the U and a court yard with latrine and water supply in the middle. The prisoners were not allowed to talk to each other and the whole system was designed to break down their will and morale.

At first there were two men in each cell, but the Communists soon discovered that they were encouraging one another so they separated them so that each man was all alone in his cell with nothing to read or do and permitted only once a day to go out, drink water and go to the latrine. Besides keeping them in solitaire their captors began to torture the men, one by one trying to make them confess atrocities against their country or to reveal military secrets. To communicate with one another, the men invented a Morse code by tapping on the walls between one cell and another.

<u>In their desperate situation, many began to turn to God for help</u>. Most were only nominal Christians, but could remember verses or snatches of the Bible. So they began to share these verses and were able to put together good portions of the Word, especially the Gospels and Psalms. When the captors discovered this, they remodeled the entire prison, making two walls between each cell so that the tapping wouldn't carry through. But God was with them and they discovered that a pipe in the cement under the doorway connected one cell to another. It was very tedious and it took 24 hours for a message to go all the way around

the cell block and back. But they were persistent and kept encouraging one another by the Scriptures.

The torturing grew more severe but the Lord sustained the men through faith. The captors tortured one man at a time. So, each one, knowing that while they were torturing him they would not be torturing the others, persisted until he couldn't stand it any longer and then invent a "confession" that anyone who knew the American culture would know it was false, like, "Babe Ruth is a terrible man and he wants to kill all the Communists and he has taught us to lie about it all!" Also, the prisoner who had the cleanup duty to clean the latrine and sweep the ground in the patio would use the broom in Morse Code to convey messages to the entire group as they would all be watching.

While these men were facing the enemy and overcoming, even though they were prisoners, there was a hidden part of the glorious church in operation. That hidden part was the prayers of the saints back home. The faithful church members who prayed. The wives and loved ones who never gave up hope and held these men before the Throne of Grace of our Lord. Only God knows and some day we will know how many things have been wrought by prayers of faith.

Some of these men were prisoners for seven years, but the captors could not manage to break even one man in spite of all their bad treatment and torture! What was the difference? The church in session, with the Word of God! Jesus was there with them! And the power of God was under girding them through the prayers of the saints back home. That was the *church* there in that dreary prison in Hanoi. Seven years and though they all came out of there very thin, not one of them had lost his mind or lost his Christian values. There were a very few among the prisoners that never did profess their faith, but they did not deter the others in their faith. The church is a marvelous living thing and the gates of hell shall not prevail against it! That prison church had no designated pastor or elders, though some were exercising leadership, <u>but it had life in Jesus our Lord!</u>

THE CHURCH IN A MINE

Thirty-three miners were trapped in a mine in Chile for 67 days and not one of them died or lost his mind. But a man was among them who was a strong Christian. He in essence became their pastor while they were there. He taught them that dying was not the worst thing that could happen to them, and they found solace in faith in God. They had a very limited amount of food and the water that dripped down into the cavern where they were trapped. The two leaders rationed out the food and they prayed. After many days the food ran out, but in two more days the drillers were able to break through with a pilot hole. What joy and hope it was to the people above when the miners sent up the message, "We are thirty three miners here and we are all alive!" When they were finally rescued, they left a message written on the wall. "We were thirty three miners trapped here for 67 days and we all got out because God was with us!"

SO THAT IS THE CHURCH, the glorious church. It can be found anywhere. It is a marvelous living thing! It's not pretentious, it's not rich, it has little power (of its own) But it has Jesus Christ in its midst and he has all power and authority in heaven and earth! It's that community of saints that love one another and read and obey the Word of God. In the glorious church, when men's traditions conflict with the Word, they obey the Word! They are not ashamed to confess that Jesus Christ is their Lord! Of course, the church in a prison and the church in the mine are not normal times churches, but God is not limited to normal times. Those churches had three things essential of the function of the glorious church; the Word of God, faith in the Living God and Jesus Christ our Lord, and Fellowship. And those three things were reality in the lives of those men and essential to their very survival!

Is the Glorious Church here today? I hope so. At least I think that should be the goal of every church body. But I fear that is not the case. Many are sleeping and many do not have that extra oil that five of the virgins lacked. I can't say that I understand how God is going to prepare the Glorious Church for his coming. It seems that it appears and disappears. In small groups and in amazing places we might find that pure fellowship and teaching of the Word.

For example, Charles Colson described that within the government of the United States and in a time when politics were very dirty, how men in high places taught him the Word, then rallied around him as a new Christian in his time of need. Things like that are repeated innumerable times in the entire world many times in situations where we would least expect to find it. The church of Philadelphia in Revelation is a model and example. If we are to take Jesus example and teaching seriously, we need to make some basic decisions about our life style and what our church should do and be. When the trumpet sounds, it's going to be too late to straighten things out! It could be that very severe persecution or natural cataclysms could help us to change pretty fast and separate those who would be willing to give their all to serve God and their fellow man.

The church in the time of the first apostles was a good example. Jesus went with them, confirming the Word they preached with signs and wonders. They adapted to every different situation. They met together in homes or borrowed buildings or in the woods or in the catacombs under Rome. They didn't go to church. They were the church!

They had no Bible schools or great institutions to support them. They had no radio or television or advertising system. New groups of Christians were thrust into difficult situations and had to stand alone, sometimes with fierce persecution. But they turned the world upside down! WHAT WILL THE GLORIOUS CHURCH DO AT THE END OF THE AGE? Jesus commanded us to "watch and pray always, that we may be accounted worthy to escape all those things that shall come to pass (the wrath of God poured out upon the earth) and _to stand_ before the Son of Man." Does that instill fear in our hearts? It should! But the apostle John tells us that perfect love drives out fear "that we may have boldness on the Day of Judgment: because as he is _so are we in this world!_" (1Jn 4:17)

Jesus Christ is coming for his bride without spot or wrinkle! Are we going to be part of that beautiful bride?

Robert F. Paden

The Plowman

ADDENDUM
KOINONIA
(FELLOWSHIP)

Fellowship (Koinonia) is part and parcel of what the church should be. The church cannot be the precious bride of Christ without it. The apostle John wrote his epistle "so that you might have *fellowship (koinonia)* with us" With whom? With those who have put their trust in Jesus for salvation! John continues, " and our fellowship is with the Father and with his Son Jesus Christ." John goes on at length to show us the <u>basis</u> of that *fellowship* ie, if we walk in the light, if we confess our sins, if we accept God's forgiveness, if we obey his commands, if we love one another, if we love not the world, if we continue and not let the antichrist seduce us, if we abide in him and live a righteous life even as Christ was righteous! (I Jn 1:1-to-2:29)

Then John goes on to show the <u>behavior</u> of fellowship and the results of living in fellowship with the Father, with his Son Jesus Christ and with one another. Jesus said, "By this shall all men know that you are my disciples, if you have love one to another!" (Jn 13:35) The apostle Paul, writes, "I beseech you that you walk worthy of the vocation wherewith ye are called, with all lowliness and meekness, with longsuffering, forbearing one another in love, endeavoring to keep the unity of the Spirit in the bond of peace." (Eph 4:1-3) The apostle Peter writes, "Seeing that you have purified your souls in obeying the truth through the Spirit unto unfeigned love of the brethren, see that ye love one another with a pure heart fervently." (I Pet 1:22) The writer of Hebrews exhorts: "Let brotherly love continue. (Heb13:1) Jude also mentions the "love feasts", warning about ungodly men creeping in and taking advantage of the confidence that Christians share with one another. Also, the very name Philadelphia means "brotherly love". That is the church the Lord promises to keep from the "hour of temptation, which will come upon the entire world to try them that dwell upon the earth." (Rev 3:10)

God's plan and purpose to build a people in which he can dwell comfortably (Eph 2:22), is shown all through the Bible, but God dwelling among us is not all of it. We must also dwell together in harmony. In fact, that is a prerequisite for our Lord to manifest his presence among us in love and power. So, we go back to what John said, "That you might have fellowship with us, and our fellowship is with the Father and his Son Jesus Christ." No one will ever know the fullness of the marvelous salvation of God without that sweet fellowship!

The fellowship of the saints is part of God's plan for building up the church. The sanctification and growth of the believers and preparing them for the battles and trials here in this life and for ruling and reigning with Christ for all eternity is in process while the brethren learn to work together, play together, pray together. This is where the action is! The work of the ministry is carried on at a personal level. Winning people to the Lord, nurturing the new born Christians, liberation, prayer and praise! It's not always an easy process. God uses the conflicts between us to humble and purify our motives. That brother or sister that's hard to get along with may be just what you need to learn to have patience, forgive, ask forgiveness when you "lose it"! In the process you may find that you are part of the problem! The testimonies of the brethren help us to see how God works and serve to inspire us in the faith. Seeing how God works in even the simplest of the believers helps us to understand how God works and helps us to trust him more.

God has not given us objects or fetishes to help us in the faith. He is invisible, but manifests himself in visible ways. We pray according to the will of God that we see in his Word and he answers us! When we realize that our Lord Jesus and our Father God heard our prayer and answered, it is so precious! He heard me and answered my prayer! That fact is more important than what we received! The Lord has given us four things to help our faith, to build the church and prepare her for his coming; (1)

his Word in the Bible, (2) prayer in the Holy Spirit, (3) the ministries; apostles, prophets, evangelists, pastors and teachers plus an example of sub ministries is given in Romans 12, (The makeup of each local church will vary according to the circumstances) (4) the fellowship of the saints. We need all four of these things to mature and build the church.

MARANATHA! HE IS COMING SOON!

About the Author

About the auth

ABOUT THE AUTHOR

Robert F Paden (The Plowman) and his wife Bettye have been in missionary service for nearly half a century. First as Short-Term Assistants in Colombia, then in church planting in Argentina. They founded and ran a Children's Home for fourteen years in which nearly 400 children were cared for and helped for long or short periods of time. Currently, Robert is working with the Wichi aborigenes in northern Argentina.

The Paden's celebrated their 65th wedding anniversary this year! They have four natural children and four adopted children, fifteen grandchildren and two great grandchildren!

Other books published by Robert are; THE KID FROM KANSAS and DECEPTION in Perilous Times.